Presented to:

_____

By:

_____

On:

_____

_____

Rainbows
IN THE NIGHT

ELAINE MARTIN

Ridgeway Publishing
Medina, NY 14103

RAINBOWS IN THE NIGHT

Copyright © 2010 by Ridgeway Publishing

Printed in Canada

*To order additional copies,
please visit your local
bookstore or contact:*

**Ridgeway Publishing
3129 Fruit Avenue
Medina, NY 14103
ph. (585) 798-0050
fax (585) 798-9016**

Cover design by M. Gagarin Design

ISBN# 978-0-9840985-5-2

Dedication

This small poem book is dedicated to all those who experience pain and suffering, especially Chronic Fatigue Syndrome, and Fibromyalgia victims.

When thou passeth through the waters, I will be with thee, and through the rivers, they shall not overflow thee. . . Isaiah 43:2

Acknowledgements

A special thank you to my parents, sisters and friends, for the encouragement given to make this book possible. May God bless you.

But He knoweth the way that
I take: when he hath tried me,
I shall come forth as gold.
Job 23:10

Nighttime Beauty

The full moon shines in splendor
On the countryside,
Its golden rays of comfort
Cheering all mankind.

These wonders of creation,
Formed by God alone,
Can draw our faint hearts closer
To our heavenly home.

The tiny stars of beauty,
Twinkling from above,
Assure that God in heaven
Looketh down with love.

Oh, welcome, precious nighttime,
Balm for weary souls,
The peace, the calm, the beauty–
God has planned it so.

Our daytime cares seem smaller,
Moonbeams shine so bright;
Dark clouds are fringed with silver
Like rainbows in the night.

Through the Waters

When thou passest through the waters
Of affliction, precious friend,
Do not faint or grow discouraged;
God is with you to the end.
> Rivers will not overflow you,
> Neither waves of sorrow drown;
> Faith in God is strength sufficient,
> He will never let you down.

Dearest friend, do not grow weary,
Though the stormy billows roll;
God Himself is still the Captain,
Guiding you through rocky shoal.
> Keep your focus on the Lighthouse--
> Jesus is the shining Star;
> He will lead you safe to heaven,
> Though the way ahead seems dark.

Keep your hand in His almighty,
Even when your faith grows dim;
Don't despair, for Jesus loves you,
Just surrender all to Him.
> God alone can bring you comfort–
> Counselor, and Prince of Peace;
> Waves are stilled at His command,
> And the mighty billows cease.

When our earthly life is over,
And we walk the heavenly shore.
We will hear our Captain whisper,
"Peace be yours forevermore."

God's Love

Crocuses are blooming,
Snow is melting fast;
Cheery robin redbreast
Has returned at last.

Little tiny blossoms,
Budding on the trees,
Await the warmer weather
And the honeybees.

Daffodils and tulips,
Sprouting from the ground,
Soon will burst with fragrance;
Colors will abound.

Precious, precious springtime!
How it shows anew,
Greatness of the Father's
Love for me and you.

Smile

Oh, let us ever day by day,
Be kind to one another
And give a friendly word to all,
To neighbor, sister, brother.

The smile is understood by all–
A language clear and plain;
Both young and old can speak it well,
Its meaning is the same.

A smile is such a little thing,
And yet it shows we care
About another's hopes and fears,
It says we want to share.

Where smiles and kindness both are found,
That is a happy place;
So let us never start our day
Without a smiling face.

What Is Love?

GOD IS LOVE

He sent to earth His own dear Son to die on Calvary,

In agony upon the cross, to set all sinners free.

FORGIVENESS IS LOVE

Did someone ruin your glad hour in unexpected way?

Can you forgive this small offense and love him anyway?

GENTLENESS IS LOVE

Gentle actions, words, or deeds soothe many a lonely heart,

While anger stirs up arguments and drives good friends apart.

PRAYER IS LOVE

How often do you kneel to pray for sorrowing, struggling friends?

When love is there, few words sincere, may bring encouragement.

UNSELFISHNESS IS LOVE

Unselfishness lets others choose the biggest and the best,

With loving thoughts, and joyfulness, content to take what's left.

THANKFULNESS IS LOVE

Thank God. When love is in our hearts, there is no greater blessing

How sad to see in Christian lives, that often it is missing.

A Baptismal Prayer

Dear Jesus, please look down upon
Thy youthful lambs tonight,
Who have exchanged their sin-sick garbs
For spotless robes of white.

They promised to be faithful, Lord,
Unto the church and Thee,
Baptismal vows were made and sealed
Today, on bended knee.

Yes, willing now to do what's right,
But still they are so young;
Oh, keep them on the narrow path
That they have just begun.

It won't be easy, Lord. Thou knowest
What all lies yet before,
Of future struggles on the way
That leads to heaven's door.

May they draw nigh to Thee, O God;
Thou art their Guide and Friend,
Almighty and omnipotent,
Thy love, Lord, has no end.

And even when the tempter comes
To lure them from their goal,
Dear Lord, I pray, please draw them close
To Thee, within the fold.

So that their hearts can molded be
With humbleness divine,
Content to fill some lowly place
As long as they are Thine.

To be the greatest and the best
Is not the heavenly key,
But meekness and submissiveness,
And yieldingness to Thee.

Help them to see it matters not
What others do or say,
But that their work is with themselves
To all Thy laws obey.

Oh, may they be a friend to all,
Love and compassion show,
For judging others is not part
Of a true Christian's goal.

We find in First Corinthians,
The chapter is thirteen–
God plainly wrote it down for man–
Just what love really means.

May they remember evermore
Faith, hope, and charity,
Yet not forgetting that love is
The greatest of these three.

Dear Jesus, bless these little lambs
And guide them on their way,
So they can meet to part no more
In heaven, some sweet day.

Controlling the Weather

Oh, the rustling of the pine trees
On a windy, warm spring day,
Tossing high the mighty branches–
Chinook breezes are at play!
　　　Swirling dust storms blowing yonder
　　　In the fields now light and dry,
　　　Faster, faster! How they're sweeping
　　　With a vengeance passing by.
Man's invented many gadgets,
Made to measure wind's own speed,
But God in heaven forms the wind
With power we can't see.
　　　Man can't once control the weather,
　　　E'en with all technology,
　　　For God omnipotent is ruling
　　　In His love and majesty.
So don't grumble if it's windy,
Or when clouds burst forth with rain.
Praise God instead—He planned it so;
Soon the sun shines bright again.
　　　There is beauty in all weather,
　　　Special treasures, rich and rare;
　　　Look for the best in every day--
　　　Wind or rain, or sunshine fair.
Because God's way is always best,
Ne'er making a mistake,
That's why I'm glad that weather machines
Are one thing man can't make!

Earthly Treasures, Heavenly Joys

It was the night before the auction of the dearest old homeplace.

The family lingered sadly, tears trickled down their face.

How precious were the memories of happy days gone by,

When Father labored long and hard, with Mother by his side.

But now the family's scattered, and the farm's put up for sale,

For Father dear is tired, and Mother's getting frail.

The farm machinery's ready, all cleaned up nice like new,

Just who will be the buyers? Oh, if we only knew!

Miscellaneous items, found around the farm,

Were loaded on a wagon, now filled with rustic charm.

There were household items too, we'd used in years before;

These things we cherished dearly, yet needed now no more.

But though these earthly treasures will scatter far and wide,

Our recollections can't be sold. (God's love did there abide.)

We always will remember the memories of the past,

A part of every heartbeat, as long as life shall last.

And though it's hard for us to see our dearest home now selling,

We all realize anew, it's just an earthly dwelling.

And now our thoughts go onward, to our heavenly home above,

Where time is never ending, and all is peace and love.

These treasures here on earth sometime will all decay,

But we'll think of them no more in heaven, some sweet day.

Joys of Autumn

Warmer summer days are passing,
One by one they're fleeting by;
Ripened grainfields now stand golden
Till glad harvesttime draws nigh.

Rows of cornstalks gently swaying
Like a sea of emerald sheen,
Whispering the song of autumn–
Rustling leaves of glossy green.

Crickets chirping in the twilight–
Hear their choruses so sweet–
Only stopping for a moment,
Followed by a soft repeat.

All the happy little faces
Of each flower blooming bright,
Linger yet, but droop their petals
When the frost hits hard one night.

See the woods with rustic colors,
Now displaying in finery
Till the wind blows down each leaflet,
Making bare the once-green tree.

Honking geese in V-formation,
Flying southward through the sky,
Off to distant warmer climates
Before wintertime draws nigh.

For these many joys of autumn,
Let's remember when we pray
To praise God, our heavenly Father,
On this glad Thanksgiving Day.

Here on earth we have four seasons–
Summer, winter, spring, and fall;
Our great God, the wise Creator,
In His goodness made them all.

Welcome, New Year

Farewell! Farewell! The old year's past,
Gone to return no more.
God in His majesty alone
Knows what lies on before.

We as His children need to trust
Our lives into His hands,
And meekly follow where He leads;
He cares and understands.

God knows how feeble poor man is;
We shrink back sore afraid
When threatening storm clouds hover nigh
Or detours change our way.

Before the problem's even close,
We worry, fret, and whine,
And wonder why God leadeth thus,
Who did our path design.

We're sure that it's impossible–
This mountain round the bend;
Oh, if we'd only then but trust
And on the Lord depend.

Instead of faltering in despair,
Let's bravely march right on,
Up to the dreaded obstacle;
Go meet it with a song.

So now at the beginning
Of a spotless, clean new year,
Let's make a resolution firm,
That we will never fear.

Let's keep our eyes upon the Saviour,
Yes, marching straight ahead,
Never wavering or doubting,
But firmly trust instead.

So even though the old year's gone
And will return no more,
Let's make this a happy new year,
E'en better than before.

Rejoice and Be Happy

Oh, let us rejoice and be happy,
Not once giving in to despair,
For Jesus, our kind, loving Shepherd,
Will help us each burden to bear.

Yes, He understands every heartache,
Knowing well the frailty of man;
And all that He asks of His children
Is to do the best that we can.

If at times you feel like a failure,
Don't think that you've failed the whole test;
But rejoice in the satisfaction
That is yours if you've done your best.

The next time just try a bit harder,
Seeking lofty goals to attain;
We dare not give way to despairing
Or thinking we tried but in vain.

Rejoice if you meet tribulation,
For the Saviour will lead you through!
What a joy to hear Jesus whisper,
"Precious child, I have need of you."

E'en though the future's uncertain,
You're afraid you won't pass the test,
Just surrender your life to Jesus;
Then all will work out for the best.

No need to be fretful or worried,
Since God is with us each day;
Instead, let us go forth rejoicing
And humbly believe and obey.

Heaven Awaits

Once more I kneel before Thee, Lord, scarce knowing what to do.

Trials and sorrows crush me low; expressive words are few.

In anguished care, my heart is torn, bowed with this anxious pain;

Tears stream down my swollen cheeks, like rivulets of rain.

Pent-up emotions in my breast are raging fierce and strong;

"I cannot, oh, I cannot, Lord, accept life and go on.

Why must I bear this awful load while others still are free?

The future path looks much too rough. Lord, must I follow Thee?"

Weary from this present battle–no one seems to care–

All alone and so forsaken, I'm sinking in despair.

Each way I turn new obstacles are looming up ahead.

"I can't see through! Oh, please, dear Lord, may I turn back instead?"

My former life few cares had known; days swiftly passed on by.

But now this burden changed it all to tears and anxious sighs.

Oh, might the Saviour have forgot His distraught child in need,

Sinking low in miry clay and wishing to be freed?

Ah, no! Dear friends, God ne'er forsakes those struggling in despair.
So tenderly He stooped down low and whispered, "Child, I care.
Precious one, rememberest thou how I died on Calvary–
Wounded, bleeding on the cross—to set all sinners free?
Gethsemane was, oh, so dark, for My disciples slept
As I faced every sinner's shame; forsaken too, I wept.
'O Father,' I did cry aloud, 'let this cup pass from Me.
Yet not My will, but Thine be done; I give My life to Thee.'
All Scripture had to be fulfilled—the whole plan of Salvation
Depended then on Me alone, for every tribe and nation.
I love thee, oh, dear child of Mine, and long to hold thee near,
To comfort thee in storms of life, to wipe away each tear.
With eager arms I'm waiting to comfort and caress,
To soothe thy wounded spirit, thy life to guide and bless.
But you must first be willing, the cross of Christ to pay.
Trusting all unto My wisdom, God's commands obey.
It's hard, dear one, (I know, oh, so well, the agony)
But remember, heaven awaits if you submit and follow Me."

Love in Action

The time to be silent is often
Just when we believe we know best--
Yes, just when we're sure we know better
Than anyone else of the rest.

When we feel there's only one answer
That really and truly is right,
It's then that we should reconsider
Instead of beginning to fight.

Take heed to the Saviour's example
And practice the Golden Rule,
As even our innocent children
Are taught to obey and to do.

Yes, do unto others as you would
Have others then do unto you.
How sad that the ones who remember
This lesson are only a few.

Compassion is love in action;
There just is no other good way
For people to see that the Saviour
Is part of your life every day.

Dear friends, let us never forget this:
That sometimes our silence is best.
Especially when we're sure that we're right,
Just simply and quietly rest.

Fading Blossoms

Come, join me now for an evening stroll
As the sun slowly sinks in the west;
My footsteps lead to the old orchard grove,
Toward the blossoming trees I love best.

Feelings of awe creep in my heart
While in wonder I gaze at the trees;
Sweet-scented perfume engulfs my nose,
From delicate fragrance blown in the breeze.

Words fail to express the genuine beauty
Of the old orchard in brilliant array;
Silhouetted distinctly as the sun sets,
This scene of perfection soon passes away.

Only a short while till blossoms droop,
Flowering petals fall to the ground;
Each in its turn floats through the air
Softly and gently without any sound.

Just like our lives in the bloom of youth–
Soon old age comes and we thrive no more.
Once-delicate petals now fading and weary,
Waiting, longing, to join friends gone before.

As life's season ends, the flower decays,
But the soul will live through eternity,
There reaping fruits of earthly labors
Forever, with immortality.

Homesick for Heaven

Dear Father in heaven, I'm weary of life,
Feeling lonesome and sad, midst this earthly strife.

My cross is so heavy, I bend neath its weight,
And long just to drop it, this miserable state.

The cup that I'm drinking is bitterly strong;
Without Thee, dear Jesus, I could not keep on.

These trials and sorrows, I don't understand,
Alone and forsaken, O God, take my hand.

I'm homesick for heaven, blest mansions on high,
To walk golden streets beyond earthly skies.

Yet I'll bravely keep on, my lifework to do,
And trust Thou wilt ever, safe carry me through.

Thy strength is sufficient, each burden to bear,
Thou art always as close as a whispered prayer.

So too, Thou wilt pilot my bark safe to shore,
For Thou hast crossed over these waters before.

The waves Thou commandedst, "Peace, peace! Be still!"
So too, I'll surrender my ALL to Thy will.

A Shut-in's Prayer

Dear Father, I thank Thee, though weakened and worn,
(My faint heart so yearns to be healthy and strong)
Thou knowest what's best and hast need of me here;
So unworthy I am, yet Thou still leadest on.

When angels of pain do envelop my frame
In the day or the night, Thy dear hand will caress
My brow in sweet solace and loving compassion.
Why should I not praise Thee for such tenderness?

I treasure the hours in Thy presence alone,
Communing with Thee in the stillness of night,
So peaceful, so tranquil. Thy love never fails;
Why shouldn't I praise Thee? Thou dost all things right.

My sickbed's a palace all shining in gold,
Surrounded with angels of comforting love.
I feel so unworthy. Why shouldn't I praise Thee
As showers of blessings come down from above?

Dear friends, don't take pity as I lie on my bed;
Pray not for less pain, but for joy in God's will.
Content not to question, for He knows what's best,
I'm trusting each hour He is with me still.

Trust and Obey

Do we strive to see life in a positive scope?

Or are negative thoughts the best way that we cope?

How sad if we see the worst in all things,

With frowning and worry that pessimism brings.

We can all choose our style: to be happy or glum;

It's not circumstances, neither rain clouds nor sun,

But our own choice of thoughts that predicts how we feel.

Our own selfish nature is a problem so real;

The big capital "I," if we can't crush it down,

Is a fast train ticket, leading into "Grump Town."

Dear friends, let us ponder what our actions portray.

Are we choosing wisely our options each day?

If we seek our own wants, we choose to be sad;

There's a much better choice: just submit and be glad!

Give your ALL unto God, and be happy all day,

For each burden seems light when we trust and obey.

A Short Span of Time

If sometimes life seems kind of dark
And our hearts are full of care,
It is such a precious comfort
To commune with God in prayer.

In the stillness of the midnight,
At the dawning of the day,
In the afternoon or evening,
Jesus hears us when we pray.

From His mighty throne in glory,
Rules the earth in majesty,
Witnessing both good and evil,
All man's actions He can see.

Every deed will be remembered.
Are we always kind and true?
Do we love each other ever,
In all that we say or do?

If we should feel that life's unfair,
Let us ponder in our heart
How very short this span of time
Till we from the earth depart.

All these petty, human worries,
That we think will never end,
Are just a portion of our life,
A short span of time to spend.

A proving time to test our faith
And see if we'll hold fast
To the blessed Rock of Ages
Till God calls us home at last.

Weary One, Look Up!

God will not leave you comfortless
Through affliction's stormy trial;
He has promised to be with you
As you walk each weary mile.

Our Father dear in heaven,
Shaped your burden with His hands,
Then chose you, faithful servant,
Out of all the nation's lands.

No one else could fill this mission,
'Twas a gentle call for thee;
God has placed this yoke upon you,
Though His reasons we can't see.

"Weary one, do not despair,"
Jesus whispers to thy soul.
"Abide with Me, be not afraid,
Though the stormy billows roll.

Precious child, I know it's hard
At this time to fully trust
While the storm in fury rages,
Blowing fierce with mighty gust.

Come closer now, dear child, to Me;
I'll keep thee safe by night and day.
Peace, be still, O fainting heart;
At last, this too shall pass away!

For even when I laid this burden
On Thy frail shoulders now to bear,
I knew its weight would well-nigh crush
Thy trembling heart into despair.

But angel hosts are watching o'er thee,
Compassionate, and tenderly
Succoring thy wounded spirit,
Always there to comfort thee.

E'en though ofttimes you wonder why,
Someday the answers will be clear.
Just take one step, then one step more.
Dear child, relax; thy Saviour's near.

I know thy own endurance level,
And I am ever in control,
Thou weary one, look up to Me!
I'll bring thee to that heavenly goal."

Faith Through Trials

Lord, Thou knowest well my weakness,
How often I fail the test:
Just to trust in faith through trials
And not question what is best.

Why this heavy burden given?
Why must I this load now bear?
Why is life so full of struggles?
Why does no one seem to care?

"Oh, dear child, I truly love you,"
Jesus whispers soft and clear.
"Just surrender all your problems;
I am with you, do not fear.

All these anxious, human worries,
That perplex your weary heart,
Some sweet day will all be answered
If My will you don't depart."

Still I pray, "Dear Lord in heaven,
Show me what I am to do,
For life's path is rough and rugged;
No one understands but You.

Well Thou knowest my desires,
Each internal, yearning plea;
Words need not in voice be spoken,
Still I trust Thou hearest me."

"Yes, indeed, My faithful follower,
Rest assured—each silent thought
That within your brave heart lingers,
Unexpressed, is known by God.

Come to Me, My yoke is easy;
I'll be with you all the way,
Though stormy waters round you rage,
Tempests billow night and day.

Oh, dear child, be true and faithful;
At life's end the crown is won,
Only if you pray sincerely,
Precious Lord, Thy will be done.' "

Fleeting Time

Day by day our lives unfolding,
Hour by hour time passes on;
God in heaven holds the stopwatch
As the minutes tick along.

Let us yield ourselves completely
To the Master's holy will,
Not rebelling where He leads us,
When the path seems all uphill.

There's a reason for each trial
That we meet with here below;
God Himself is the conductor,
Though the way we do not know.

Peace comes with a full surrender
Of a meek and contrite heart;
Only then will we be ready
When from earth we may depart.

Someday God shall halt our stopwatch,
And eternity must come;
Our reward will last forever
If the Master says, "Well done."

A Loved One Gone Before

When your heart feels sad and lonely
With sorrow's numbing pain,
And your life cross seems so heavy,
You can never smile again.

Oh, dear friend, do not grow weary
With the battle now at hand,
For you have the blest assurance
That it is the Master's plan.

God is with you in the valley,
You are never there alone;
Though the path be rough and winding,
Still He guides His children home.

When your eyes with tears are blinded
As you think of bygone days,
Just keep clinging to the Master,
Trusting in His perfect ways.

This is but a little time span,
Now dividing hearts in twain,
Some sweet day to be united,
Never more to part again.

Until then, just keep on trusting,
Even on life's stormy sea;
'Twill be worth each sigh and teardrop
When God calls, "Come unto Me."

Hope for Tomorrow

My heart is torn with anguish, Lord. I need Your helping hand;
Trials and cares come thronging fast upon this weary land.

Present troubles crush me low, dear Father—this Thy will.

Thou knowest why it must be so. O restless heart, be still.

The path before looks dark and drear; no light ahead I see.

Not my will, Lord, but Thine be done; I give my life to Thee.

All hopes and dreams are gone, O God; with tears my eyes o'erflow.

This fainting heart cries out to You, Why must I suffer so?

"My precious child, you're not alone; I know this present pain,

Is sinking you nigh to despair; your life seems all in vain.

Dear little lamb, I love you so, come closer now to Me.

These darkened shadows soon will pass; the morning you shall see.

Lean hard on Me, dear weary one; relax within My care.

Lift up thy tear-stained face, and kneel in humble, trusting prayer."

"Dear Lord, I come with broken heart; surrendered to Thy will.

I'm ready to obey command, I'll pause and just keep still.

"Dear faithful one, I know it's hard, to rest in patience sweet,

The busy world goes rushing past with strength full and complete.

But child of Mine, I needed thee. No one the whole world through

Could carry now this present pain; 'twas molded just for you.

Fight on once more, brave little heart, through trials, cares, and sorrow,

Rejoicing ever in the hope of a better day tomorrow."

Contentment

Contentment is a virtue
We all should strive to seek.
It shows complete submission
And joy at Jesus' feet.

It never looks to others
With bitter jealousy,
Comparing circumstances
That cannot altered be.

Contentment shows in action
The words, "Thy will be done,"
Combined with gentle meekness
That glorifies God's Son.

No stinging words of mockery
Will lash out at a friend,
Since kindness, too, is part of
A life that is content.

O Lord, bless all who practice
These virtues day by day,
To live in true contentment
And all Thy laws obey.

Let It Rest

If we could see inside the hearts
Of friends and family dear,
To fully understand their lives
Each joy and anxious tear,

I wonder if we'd pause a bit
Instead of wrongly judge
The failures that we thought were theirs
And bothered us so much.

If I were you and you were me
For only just one day–
Exchanging one another's cross–
I wonder what we'd say.

But since it is not possible
To trade the lives of men,
Let's follow firm the Golden Rule
And see what happens then.

'Tis sure that when our hearts are filled
With love for one and all,
We'll see the best in everyone
Who heeds the Saviour's call.

E'en though things are not always done
How we think would be best,
Be still! And don't unfairly judge,
But let the matter rest.

Our Life Is on Record

Every morning when we waken,
Let us give the Lord our hand,
Meekly follow where He leads us,
Though we may not understand.

Let our hearts be filled with gladness
And our cup with joy o'er flow,
As we count our many blessings
That the Lord on us bestows.

Never stopping for a moment
To discern if life seems fair,
May we humbly follow Jesus;
We are safe within His care.

Precious day the Lord has given,
Ne'er another quite the same;
It is up to us to use it
To the glory of His Name.

All the words that we have spoken,
Every thought within our head,
Will someday be laid before us
When the Judgment book is read.

Let us always practice kindness
As our earthly life we trod,
For each action is recorded
In the Autograph of God.

The Difference

One morning I woke, feeling grumpy and blue;

My thoughts were all muddled, my blessings seemed few.

Each person I met, all through the long day,

Seemed to scowl back at me and had little to say.

The next morning came round, and I jumped out of bed,

With a smile on my face and good thoughts in my head.

Each comrade I talked with now shared in my joy;

The hours passed swiftly, not one thing did annoy.

Dear friends, what a difference there is to be had

When a thought life is altered from grumpy to glad!

We should daily ask Jesus to help us be cheery;

With Him there is sunshine; not one day seems dreary.

With all of us seeking for joy all day long,

Our lives will be happy, our hearts full of song.

Strength for Each Moment

When life's troubles loom before us,
And our lot seems hard to bear,
And the threatening clouds of chaos
Almost make our hearts despair.
Oh, 'tis then we dare not waver,
Clinging still to God's own hand,
In faith committing earthly cares
To the Master's holy plan.
It is His will that man can't see
Life's pathway of tomorrow,
Knowing not what will befall us,
If it be of joy or sorrow.
For these things don't really matter,
Since His way is always best;
If we seek God's will sincerely,
He will help us pass the test.
Our Lord will grant sufficient strength
For each trial of today,
But future weeks and months and years,
Yet are veiled from life's pathway.
All that God asks of you and me
Is to humbly do His will,
And not worry 'bout the future,
For He will be with us still.

Be Still

"Be still, and know that I am God."
This message yet is true;
The Bible says to wait on Him
Until He shows us what to do.

We, the clay, must first be molded
With the Potter's careful hand;
Then we're led through fiery trials
Only God can understand.

If our faith is put to question,
Can't we trust and just be still?
Looking not for greener pastures,
Calm, serene, within God's will.

If the path be rough and rugged,
And the sun we cannot see,
Help us, Lord, e'en then to wait,
Submissive, trusting all to Thee.

Infinite Peace

There is a peace that passeth understanding,
A confidence and faith that God is near.
Our hearts can tell, that all is well,
If we just trust in Him and never fear.

There is a calm that cometh after storm clouds,
A rainbow promising God's love secure,
While arching high, up in the sky,
Its colors shining radiant and pure.

There is a joy that fills our hearts with singing,
Triumphant and rejoicing every day;
Christ died for all, who heed His call
And follow Him along the narrow way.

There is a hope of God's celestial promise,
A quiet longing, yearning to be there,
With Him above, where all is love,
And gone forever is all earthly care.

There is a race that must be run with patience,
Our life on earth is but a fleeting thing;
We'll do our best, leave God the rest,
And live each day to serve our Lord and King.

There is a place where time is never ending,
In heaven there is sweet tranquility;
I pray we'll meet, at Jesus' feet,
And dwell with Him in immortality.

Joy in Submission

Why is it thus that in our lives
We struggle hard and long
Till we submit to God's own will,
Once more to Him belong?

It seems we think our ways are best,
And we rebel at first;
When God leads us to thorny paths,
We promptly think the worst.

Faith, contentment, and submission
Have vanished from our heart;
And miserable, we wonder if
God will from us depart.

How very sad when we are thus
Rebelling against God's plan,
He who created all things well
With His almighty hand.

Oh, let us never hesitate
To follow God's own will,
For even in the future day
He will be with us still.

Oh, let's renew our faith in God
And trust Him evermore.
Yes, just surrender and submit
To God's ways that lie before.

The Sunset's Glow

When the sun sets in the evening
On a peaceful, quiet night,
Let us pause for just a moment
To behold this lovely sight.

Oh, just see the pastel colors,
Intertwined with vivid blue.
Then as twilight shadows deepen,
Now the sun must bid adieu.

Oh, this precious hour is priceless!
Naught on earth can quite compare
To this tranquil benediction,
Like a solemn evening prayer.

Lift your eyes unto the heavens,
Feel your heart from care set free,
As you pause in silent wonder
And behold God's majesty.

Weary hearts are then drawn closer
To the loving Lord on high,
As we feel His shining presence
Silhouetted in the sky.

Pity those who are too busy
With their work that's never done,
And can't pause for just a moment
To behold the setting sun.

39

Surrender

S oftly, sweetly, surrender flows
    Inside a broken heart;
U nto the Lord, our all is given,
    Self-will must now depart.

R eady to lay down pride and fame,
    Exchanged for sacrifice,
R eady to walk Surrender Road–
    A lowly, humble life.

E nter the strait and narrow way,
    With Jesus as the Guide.
N ow comes contentment, peace within,
    For God is at our side.

D o not despair when shadows fall
    Across Surrender Road.
E fforts of yours might seem in vain;
    You're crushed beneath the load.

R emember yet, dear friend of mine,
    Surrender is still the best,
    For heaven will be worth it all
    If we don't fail this test.

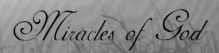

Miracles of God

Oh, these balmy summer evenings
Have a sweetness all their own–
Golden grain is softly swaying,
With the breezes gently blown.

Stalks of corn reach for the sunshine,
Hayfields drying in the heat,
Birdies warbling in the treetops,
Hushing now the world to sleep.

Flowers blooming bright and cheery,
Close their petals for the night,
Trusting that the Master Gardener,
In the morning bringeth light.

We as humans plant small seedlings,
Trusting that the Lord, with love,
Will provide both rain and sunshine,
Daily blessings from above.

Far too oft we take for granted,
When we sow beneath the sod,
That the fruits of all our labors
Are the miracles of God.

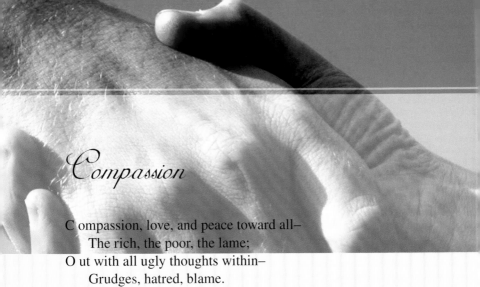

Compassion

C ompassion, love, and peace toward all–
    The rich, the poor, the lame;
O ut with all ugly thoughts within–
    Grudges, hatred, blame.

M ake room for kindliness instead;
    Be good to all you meet,
P runing first your own shortcomings,
    Humbly at Jesus' feet.

A sking prayerfully for mercy,
    The failures look so big!
S elfish motives, boastful jesting . . .
    My heart indeed looks sick.

S uch a mess within my bosom;
    I've sunk down very low.
I pray, "Dear Lord, please help me,
    These awful thoughts must go."

O nly having sweet compassion
    Within this heart of mine,
N ever seeking faults in others,
    But rather self refine.

Don't

Whenever you feel like complaining
About some fault of another,
Don't yield to this awful temptation,
Be it neighbor or sister or brother.

Unkind words have a magnetic force,
Pulling one way—back to you.
Till the circle's completed and done,
It's yourself, with faults quite a few!

There's a much better plan for us all:
Speak loving and kind every day.
Then when echoes of words come back,
We'll never be filled with dismay.

Rainbow of Friendship

True friends are like rainbows,
Bringing hope to the heart,
In the midst of life's storm clouds,
Rays of cheer will impart.

Though raindrops are falling
Like tears from the eyes,
A true friend sees the rainbow
Overhead in the skies.

Like a beacon of faith,
Shining softly and pure,
Arching high in the heavens,
Blessed promise secure.

"A symbol of comfort,"
My friend whispers to me.
"In the midst of your burdens,
There is solace for thee."

Oh, rainbow of friendship,
May it never grow dim,
But keep glowing forever
In our hearts deep within.

A Thankful Heart

When we wake up in the morning,
Let us thank the Lord for rest,
Then give all we meet a greeting
And just smile our very best.

Do willingly the job that's ours,
Never grumble or complain;
Others read our inner thought lives,
For our actions show them plain.

Let's remember to act kindly,
Be a friend to all we meet,
Lend a helping hand so gladly
To each one who is in need.

So when the day departeth
At setting of the sun,
We will be glad within our heart
For each loving deed we've done.

The Road Map to Heaven

Our road map and our compass,
Are held by God's own hand;
We follow His directions,
Though we don't understand.

He leads us through the valleys,
Then over hills so high,
And unexpected detours,
That tempt us to ask, "Why?"

This road that we are traveling
Is but a one-way street;
The compass points us forward,
Our steps can ne'er retreat.

Just when our journey endeth
Is not for us to know
Until the map and compass,
Direction no more show.

When these are still and silent,
We've reached our heavenly goal;
Our race of life now over–
God led us safely home!